Dentist Tools

by Laura Hamilton Waxman

BUMBA BOOKS™

LERNER PUBLICATIONS ◆ MINNEAPOLIS

Note to Educators

Throughout this book, you'll find critical-thinking questions. These can be used to engage young readers in thinking critically about the topic and in using the text and photos to do so.

Lerner Publications Company
A division of Lerner Publishing Group, Inc.
241 First Avenue North
Minneapolis, MN 55401 USA

For reading levels and more information, look up this title at www.lernerbooks.com.

Main body text set in Helvetica Textbook Com Roman 23/49.
Typeface provided by Linotype AG.

Library of Congress Cataloging-in-Publication Data

Names: Waxman, Laura Hamilton.
Title: Dentist tools / Laura Hamilton Waxman.
Description: Minneapolis : Lerner Publications, [2019] | Series: Bumba books. Community helpers tools of the trade | Audience: Age 4–7. | Audience: Grade K to 3. | Includes bibliographical references and index.
Identifiers: LCCN 2018033624 (print) | LCCN 2018039492 (ebook) | ISBN 9781541556515 (eb pdf) | ISBN 9781541555600 (lb : alk. paper)
Subjects: LCSH: Dentistry—Juvenile literature. | Dental instruments and apparatus—Juvenile literature. | Teeth—Care and hygiene—Juvenile literature.
Classification: LCC RK63 (ebook) | LCC RK63 .W39 2019 (print) | DDC 617.6—dc23

LC record available at https://lccn.loc.gov/2018033624

Manufactured in the United States of America
1-46015-42932-10/22/2018

Table of
Contents

Let's Visit the Dentist!

A dentist uses tools to check and

clean your teeth.

She helps keep your mouth healthy.

A patient is a person who

visits the dentist.

Patients sit in a special chair.

A dentist checks your teeth and gums.

He wears a mask and gloves.

Why do you think dentists wear masks and gloves?

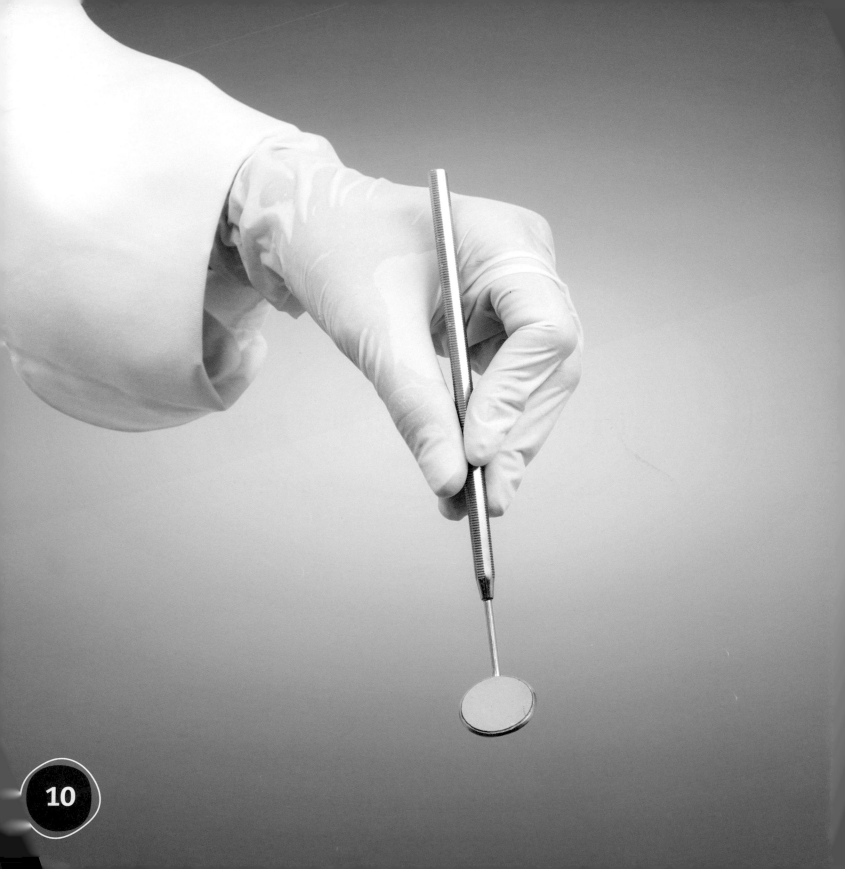

The dentist uses a mouth mirror.

It shows deep inside your mouth.

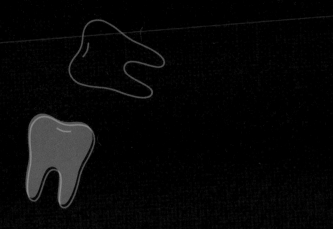

The dentist uses a scraper too.

This tool helps clean your teeth.

How do you clean your teeth at home?

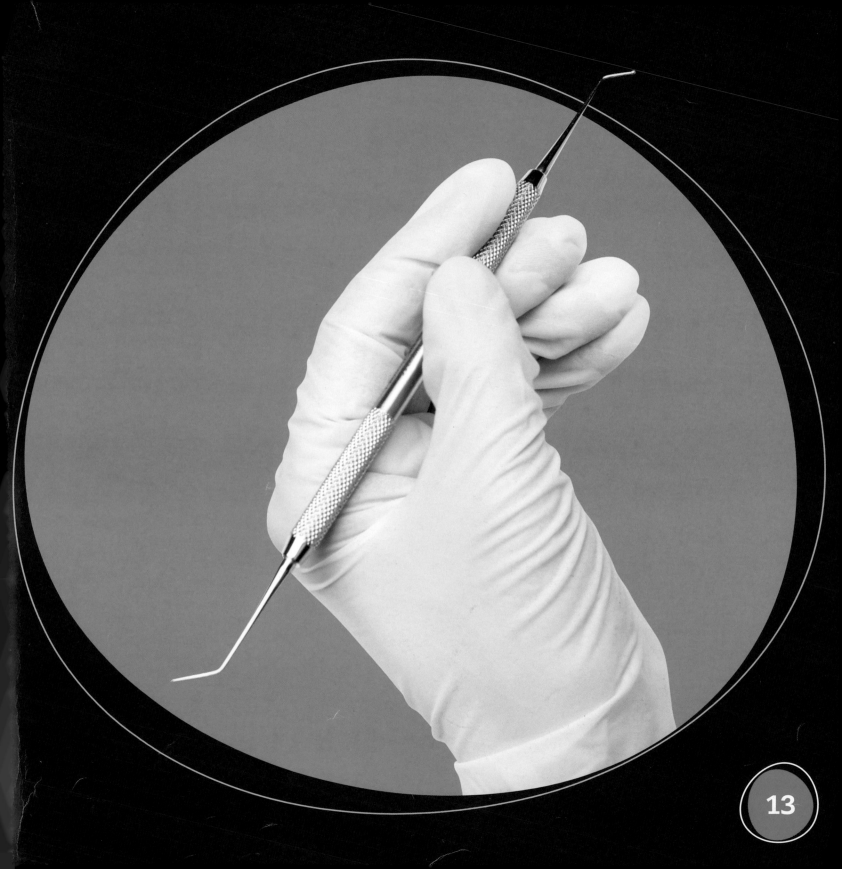

13

Floss fits in tight spaces.

It cleans between teeth.

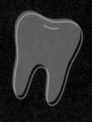

The dentist may take X-rays.

X-rays show the inside of your teeth.

They show if you have a cavity.

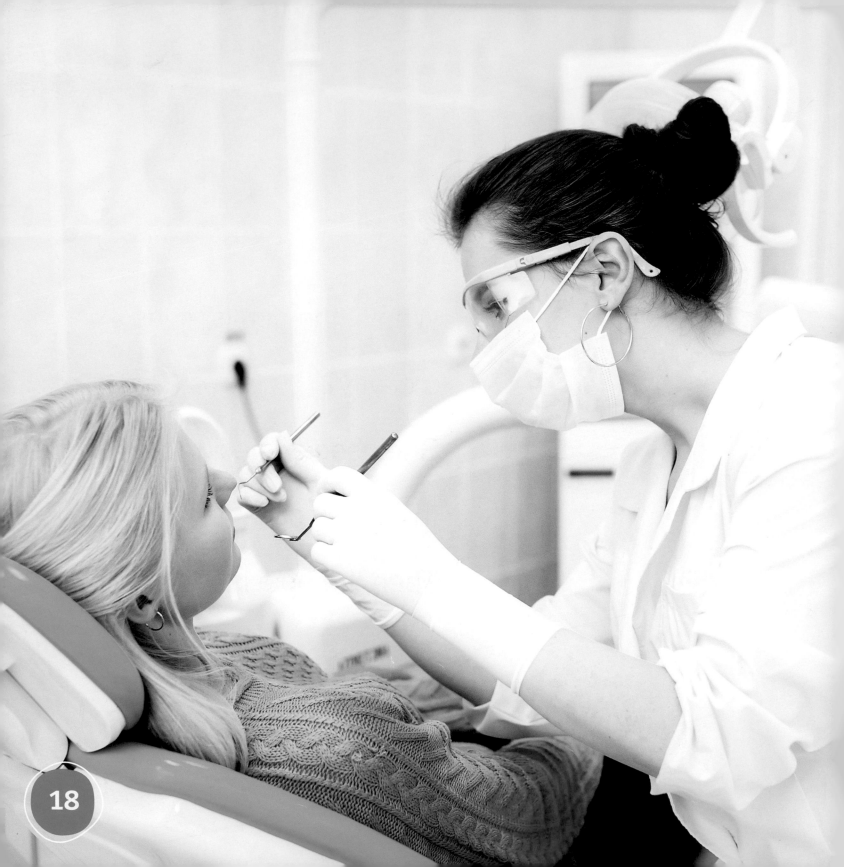

What if the dentist finds

a cavity?

She uses a special tool

to clean it out.

Then the hole is filled.

A dentist may give you a

toothbrush and floss.

You can keep your teeth

healthy at home.

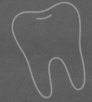

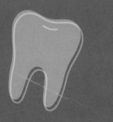

Dentist Tools

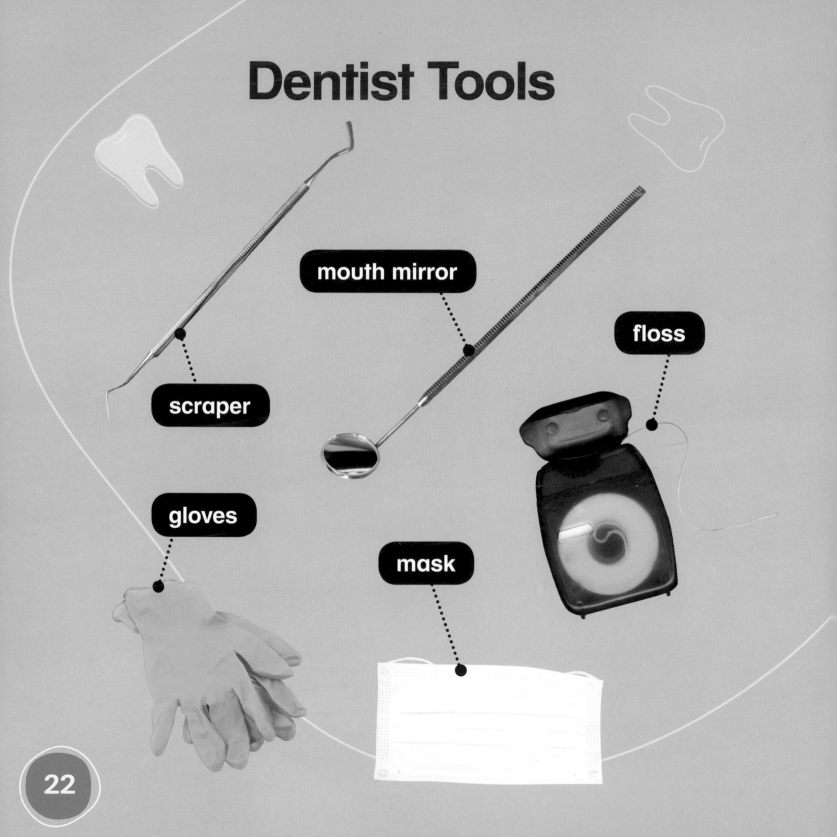

mouth mirror

scraper

floss

gloves

mask

Picture Glossary

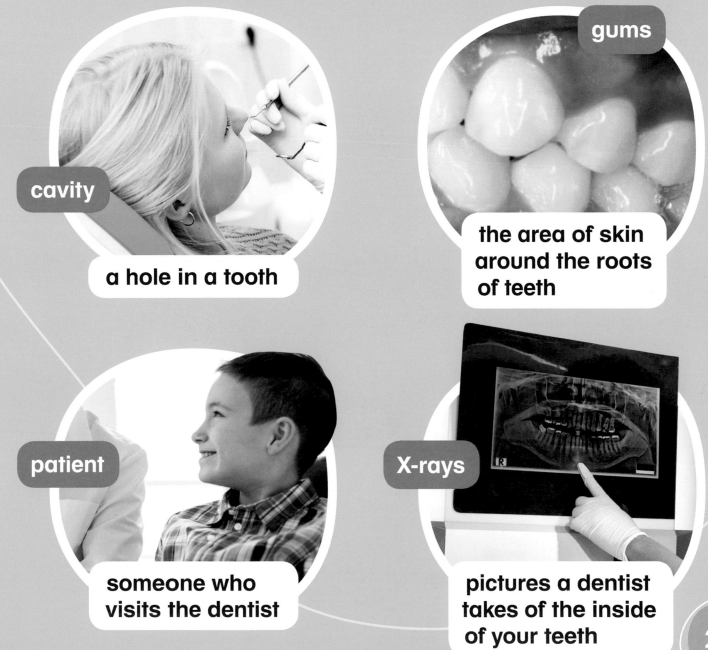

cavity

a hole in a tooth

gums

the area of skin around the roots of teeth

patient

someone who visits the dentist

X-rays

pictures a dentist takes of the inside of your teeth

23

Read More

Clark, Rosalyn. *Why We Go to the Dentist.* Minneapolis: Lerner Publications, 2018.

Kenan, Tessa. *Hooray for Dentists!* Minneapolis: Lerner Publications, 2018.

Schuh, Mari C. *Dentists.* Minneapolis: Bellwether Media, 2018.

Index

Photo Credits

Image credits: ARLOU_ANDREI/Shutterstock.com, p. 5; Syda Productions/Shutterstock.com, pp. 6, 23; Nestor Rizhniak/Shutterstock.com, p. 9; artist/Shutterstock.com, p. 10; Pixel-Shot/Shutterstock.com, p. 12; Bill Varie/Getty Images, p. 15; AtnoYdur/Getty Images, pp. 16, 23; Aliaksandr Barouski/Shutterstock.com, pp. 19, 23; Stas Malyarevsky/Shutterstock.com, p. 21; Pop Paul-Catalin/Shutterstock.com, p. 22; Luis Carlos Torres/Shutterstock.com, p. 22; kourafas5/Getty Images, p. 22; Sergey Mironov/Shutterstock.com, p. 23; KHANISTHA SRIDONCHAN/Shutterstock.com, p. 23.

Cover Images: wavebreakmedia/Shutterstock.com; Africa Studio/Shutterstock.com.